OUR OWN WORLD

SRISTEE KAPIL

Copyright © Sristee Kapil
All Rights Reserved.

This book has been self-published with all reasonable efforts taken to make the material error-free by the author. No part of this book shall be used, reproduced in any manner whatsoever without written permission from the author, except in the case of brief quotations embodied in critical articles and reviews.

The Author of this book is solely responsible and liable for its content including but not limited to the views, representations, descriptions, statements, information, opinions and references ["Content"]. The Content of this book shall not constitute or be construed or deemed to reflect the opinion or expression of the Publisher or Editor. Neither the Publisher nor Editor endorse or approve the Content of this book or guarantee the reliability, accuracy or completeness of the Content published herein and do not make any representations or warranties of any kind, express or implied, including but not limited to the implied warranties of merchantability, fitness for a particular purpose. The Publisher and Editor shall not be liable whatsoever for any errors, omissions, whether such errors or omissions result from negligence, accident, or any other cause or claims for loss or damages of any kind, including without limitation, indirect or consequential loss or damage arising out of use, inability to use, or about the reliability, accuracy or sufficiency of the information contained in this book.

Made with ♥ on the Notion Press Platform
www.notionpress.com

Contents

1. For The First Time..- Sristee Kapil	1
2. Favorite Or Right- Sristee Kapil	3
3. Second Time Love- Shreya Singh	5
4. Our Own World- Dakshita Gangwar	7
5. What Makes Me Happy- Shria Chirvi	9
6. In A Field Of Sunflower- Singamsetty Nachiketa	12
7. The Boy Within-Singamsetty Nachiketa	14
8. The Boundless Storyteller- Singamsetty Nachiketa	16
9. A Fairytale Rewritten- Singamsetty Nachiketa	18
10. Hug- Daksh Jain	20
11. Night- Daksh Jain	22
12. Love- Daksh Jain	24
13. Pearl- Daksh Jain	26
14. Why?- Daksh Jain	28
15. Passing By- Daniel Yumkham	30
16. Unrequited Constellations- Shaaz	32
17. Timeless Love- Ahana Banerjee	34
18. Light Green Eyes- Angel Rathi	36
19. Somcone All Mine- Angel Rathi	38
20. Forever By Your Side- Angel Rathi	40
21. In All I Love- Angel Rathi	42
22. The Weight Of Dying Petals- Gyayak Jain	44
23. Love In The Distance- Gyayak Jain	46
24. Fated To Fade- Gyayak Jain	48

Contents

25. A Love That Never Fades- Gyayak Jain	51
26. The Dream Eve- Akshat Shevde	54
27. Jealous- Akshat Shevde	56
28. The Backup- Akshat Shevde	57
29. Fear Of Attachments- Akshat Shevde	59
30. Love - Gargi Singh	61
31. Mine- Gargi Singh	63
32. I Give You- Gargi Singh	64
33. "O' Krishna, My Lord Of This World"- Shivang Maurya	66
34. You're My Everything- Priyanka Pandit	68
35. Hey!- Mobin	69
36. Flames That Flickers- R. Subash Sai Sudhan	70
37. Promise Made- R. Subash Sai Sudhan	71
38. Forever Yours, Never Mine- Sanvi Jaiswal	72
39. Love Is Not A Game- Joy Pannu	74
40. I Hate Roses- Chrysolyte	75
41. The One That Got Away- Suhana Saha	77
42. One Heart, One Soul- Lovejeet Sharma	79

1. For the first time..- Sristee kapil

SRISTEE KAPIL

BIO- A 20 year old, who just loves to depict her emotions through her poetry.

Instagram- *@sristee_writezz*

For the first time, i opened my eyes,
I saw his face & forgot that i was crying,
He came near me & i saw his charm,
For the first time, a father held his daughter in his arms,
I don't know why but i suddenly felt calm,
For the first time, a baby girl smiled,
But i was amazed that his smile was way brighter than mine,
It felt like, i got what i wanted from my life,
A father, who knew that his love is all his little baby girl wants,
But then i grew up & that's when life threw the dice,
Then for the first time, i cried & kept crying,
But this time he didn't came & smiled,
& The chaos inside me kept thriving,
Or may be it was just craving for those arms,
To hold me tight & let me cry as much as i want,
For the first time, that baby girl craved this hard,

Not for anything else but for her father's charm,

2. Favorite or Right- Sristee kapil

SRISTEE KAPIL

BIO- *A 20 year old, who just loves to depict her emotions through her poetry.*

Instagram- *@sristee_writezz*

"For once in a life we have to go through a never ending fight,
Which is either to choose our favorite or the things which are right,
It's not enough easy as it looks,
One is what make us happy and another is a truth,
But is it okay to die our soul for the things which makes you sad but are right,
It's not compulsory to always go for the one which is right,
I may sound selfish,
But what's wrong in living our life by our wish,
Being right fo matters but first be the right one for yourself then make other's day bright,
Otherwise you will be burdened by your own soul & loose it's all shine,
Sometimes doing the favorite is okay if it brings you a smile,

Just imagine what's the point of life if you didn't learned how to become your own smile"

3. Second Time Love- shreya singh

SHREYA SINGH

Bio - *I am shreya singh, an 18 year old. And i love writing poems , ,through my poetry i love expressing myself. I believe pthers would also find my poem relatable and peaceful !!*
Instagram– *poetryaa_27_*

******

Let's talk about , what
gives you another hope.
And makes your life glow again.
They healed the pain,
which was never given by them
It was mature, had deeper understanding
And had deeper insecurity
Will it be the same as the first?
Whether I will be left alone again?
The scars and pain endured in the past
Makes you question their every action.
But it is they who help you,
break free from your shell
When you are an over thinker

They become an over explainer
They are the lamp of your life
When you are in the house of darkness
They are the reason you believe
Yes, things can be resolved!

4. Our Own World- dakshita gangwar

DAKSHITA GANGWAR

Bio - I am a 20 old year medical student who have passion of writing and also painting .I started writing at the age of 12 . I want to share my aspects of life to the world through my writings.
Instagram *– dakshita_gangwar*

******

My hands shivers down ,
The realisation hit me like a clown ,
It was not a cold weather ,
But my heart felt like feather ,
Time when I get to know ,
This is last time when ,
I open my eyes and you Show ,
My ocean filled eyes ,
Trying to capture your blurry image ,
Some sadness ached in my heart ,
And my mind get filled with rage ,
I can't accept I lost you ,
But you were never mine ,
My adult understanding accepted it ,

But childishness thought you are divine,
Yes My fate snatched you from me,
But you're the only thing my dreams see,
You're image is the last seen one,
Before I fell asleep to rising sun,
The moon became my bestfriend,
It's the only one who listen at the end,
I start bleeding on pen and paper,
People appreciated you'll be good rapper,
My life getting at its ups,
But my loneliness sucks,
This is not what I wanted,
My inner self is haunted,
Without you my world is dull,
Let's meet in OUR OWN WORLD.

5. What Makes Me Happy- shria chirvi

SHRIA CHIRVI

***Bio** - Shria Chirvi, born on 22 March, 2007, is a talented poet hailing from the picturesque region of Jammu and Kashmir. From a young age, she exhibited a profound ability to express intricate human emotions through her poetry, skillfully blending imagination with subtlety. What began as a mere hobby blossomed into an inseparable aspect of her identity, as words wove themselves intricately into the fabric of her life. Shria's deep reverence for nature and her passion for dancing are palpable themes that resonate throughout her poetic repertoire, lending a unique and vibrant flavor to her verses. Her literary prowess has not gone unnoticed, with her works finding a place in various anthologies, further cementing her status as a rising star in the world of poetry. Through her evocative words, Shria continues to captivate hearts and minds, leaving an indelible mark on the literary landscape.*
Instagram *– shria03*

******

They ask,
"What makes you smile, what makes your heart sing?

Is it love, is it laughter, or some other thing?"
I chuckle, because how do i explain
that joy sometimes hides in the middle of rain?
Not the storm, not the thunder's loud call,
but in rainbows that arch, after it all.
It's in that sweet, slow, romantic song,
where i twirl by myself, but it doesn't feel wrong,
I dance like a dream, no one else in sight,
spinning so fast i'm almost in flight.
No drinks, no buzz, just the music and me,
feeling high on my own kind of glee,
Lying on the floor, breath catching in my chest,
I listen to my heartbeat, steady & blessed,
it's like a secret drum playing just for me,
Reminding me of life's soft melody,
And oh my brother- what joy he brings!
We laugh over nothing, over the silliest things,
Snapchat filters turns us into dogs with hats,
because honestly. who needs serious chats?
Our talks run deep, but the jokes runs deeper,
and those moments make happiness feel sweeter,
Momos?Don't get me started on these
each bite like a hug wrapped in warm,doughy clothes.
And those rides that twist, and make me scream?
They turn fear into joy, like a childhood dream.
I smile at jhumkas, sparkling, dancing as I walk,
rings on my fingers that glitter as I talk.

Bollywood romance, cheesy but grand,
where love conquers all with a song and a hand.
Maybe life's not a movie, but sometimes I wish,
for a love story that ends with a Bollywood kiss.
Poetry flows, like rain on a page,
spilling my thoughts, line after line,
capturing the moments, the feeling, the rage,
turning life's chaos into something divine.
Happiness isn't one thing, it's a burst of many,
rainbows & laughter, and jokes shared with any,
It's dances with myself, rides that makes me scream,
momos & memories that feels like a dream,
In every small thing, joy quietly hides,
In laughter with my brother or rain soaked rides,
And as i lie there, heartbeat under my hand,
I smile knowing this joy needs no grand plan,
It's life, it's love, it's these everyday things,
the heartbeat, the laughter, the moments that sing.

6. In a field of sunflower- singamsetty nachiketa

SINGAMSETTY NACHIKETA

***BIO** - I am a student who loves the world of stories, literature and poetry. I am just here to share my heart and mind, hoping to help someone else put their feelings into words.*

***Instagram** - @boylovdsummer*

In a field of Sunflowers,
She is a queen among them,
Adored by both the dawn and the dusk,
And lastly, a little boy.
Adorned with a golden crown,
She sways in the wind,
Making the wind blush.
The boy cherished her.
In a field of Sunflowers,
He loved her the most.
She radiated the light of the sun,
Her presence stirring the earth,
Making the little boy's heart skip several spaces.
The boy doesn't recall why it happened, or how he fell for her,
Because in a field of Sunflowers,

he was drawn to her sun-drenched petals and
He loved her the most.
but in his quiet heart, a whispered echoed
"Am I cherished too?".
The boy was confused.
His heart, a mighty fortress,
Has always kept it's walls closed,
not to give it away to
any gorgeous daffodil or the humble daisy.
Not even the handsome dahlia nor
The beautiful lavender ever managed to stir him from his solitude.
But here, in a field of Sunflowers,
his heart softened in her light,
melting the frost away and his heart,
was not a mighty fortress anymore.
In a field of sunflowers,
He loved her the most and
She was his muse.

7. The boy within- Singamsetty nachiketa

SINGAMSETTY NACHIKETA

***BIO** - I am a student who loves the world of stories, literature and poetry. I am just here to share my heart and mind, hoping to help someone else put their feelings into words.*

***Instagram** - @boylovdsummer*

But I was just a boy once again
Walking alone, hoping to dance again.
When I lay on my unwelcoming bed,
I covered myself, wishing for a home,
Hoping the demons wouldn't find me.
Little did I know, the demons curled beside me,
Their whispers cold, wrapping me tight.
I lay there wishing tomorrow wouldn't come,
And tried to hide him—the boy—
Because he felt deeply, too deeply.
If he stayed the same,
A rainstorm would spill from his heart,
Drowning him in sorrow and fear.

His tears would soak the earth below,
Leaving him lost, yearning for relief.
But somewhere, deep inside, a light remained,
Flickering softly, calling his name.
He stood up slowly, weary but strong,
Knowing that even in the darkest night,
The boy within could still belong.

8. The Boundless Storyteller- singamsetty nachiketa

SINGAMSETTY NACHIKETA

BIO - I am a student who loves the world of stories, literature and poetry. I am just here to share my heart and mind, hoping to help someone else put their feelings into words.

Instagram- *@boylovdsummer*

Once upon a time,
in distant lands, a boy was born.
His heart, sworn to fables of old,
Tales of glory and stories of love.
Each night, his mother spun tales of the heart,
While his father spoke of unsung warriors.
The boy wove a rich world beneath his eyelids,
And every night, his dreams took flight.
As winters came and went,
The boy discovered stories had no borders.
He listened to voice near and voices far,
And for him, no language was strange to hear.
Now, stories rest at his fingertips,

Voices from around the world converge.
In every soul, he finds a chapter,
As he begins to write his own.

9. A Fairytale Rewritten- singamsetty nachiketa

SINGAMSETTY NACHIKETA

***BIO**- I am a student who loves the world of stories, literature and poetry. I am just here to share my heart and mind, hoping to help someone else put their feelings into words.*

***Instagram** - @boylovdsummer*

If we ever meet in a faraway land,
A land much like a fairytale,
With castles in the sky and rivers of gold,
Completely foreign and new,
And they never knew us together,
Can we begin anew? Can we
Rewrite our story in this fairytale,
Paint a story with a much
Different palette of colours?
The painting will remind us of our old
Hues— Shades of blue and grey—
and if the winds whisper in that distant land,
With songs we've never heard before,
Would we dare to dance beneath the stars,
With lighter steps than ever before?

Could we find each other once again,
In the spaces between dream and waking,
Where only magic lingers in the air?
But would we dare to begin again,
With hearts unburdened and free.
Just you and me?
Just us, once again.

10. Hug- daksh jain

DAKSH JAIN

BIO- As a Computer Science Engineering student, venturing into the world of authorship has been a fulfilling experience. My writings offer diverse perspectives on life, inviting readers to explore the intricacies of human experience. I Invite fellow writers, readers, and professionals, and welcome your thoughts on this new endeavor. I find solace and inspiration in the world of literature...

Instagram - @word_by_soul

When i fell into those arms,
The arms of the only special one,
I didn't know it was the last alarm....
When i saw the one replaced by none....
The soul melted by the heat,
But the pain cooled down to tears,
That hug made my heart beat...
And the voice blessed my ears.....
Lost that love, care and affection,
In just a day, with one last breath,
Lost that voice which made the correction...
In just a day, with one healing to depth....
Finding the special one in the crowd,

Still my arms crave the arms on the hearthrug,
After knowing the arms are in the shroud...
And for forever i lost the special hug....

11. Night- daksh jain

DAKSH JAIN
BIO- *As a Computer Science Engineering student, venturing into the world of authorship has been a fulfilling experience. My writings offer diverse perspectives on life, inviting readers to explore the intricacies of human experience. I Invite fellow writers, readers, and professionals, and welcome your thoughts on this new endeavor. I find solace and inspiration in the world of literature...*
Instagram- *@word_by_soul*

Just as the sun sinks,
Not a time but an era blinks,
Holding the dark,
Of sorrow and the old mark,
Comes not just to tease,
But it brings the pain on lease,
Makes us suffer with complete fear,
And we realise the absence of one to hear,
Hold the curse of our mistakes,
But have to accept it without retakes,
We have to fight and say it to stop,
Only we and we can learn to top,
Nothing can make us scare,

And can't stop for us to care,
Let's stand again with the rising sun,
Every morning with lots of fun.....

12. Love- daksh jain

DAKSH JAIN

BIO- *As a Computer Science Engineering student, venturing into the world of authorship has been a fulfilling experience. My writings offer diverse perspectives on life, inviting readers to explore the intricacies of human experience. I Invite fellow writers, readers, and professionals, and welcome your thoughts on this new endeavor. I find solace and inspiration in the world of literature...*

Instagram- *@word_by_soul*

Let me be the special one to feel
Making you the only source to heal,
Let me drown in those brown eyes
Just as deep as the ocean and skies...
Let me be the special one to host
You being smart and you like a ghost,
You and your true side, let me see
In front of me but not as me....
Let me be the special one to heart
By your side and still apart
Let me die for that special smile
Hurting my heart as a missile..

Let me be the special one to hold
Not only you but your old
Let me have your reply
With no rules to apply...

13. Pearl- daksh jain

DAKSH JAIN

***BIO**- As a Computer Science Engineering student, venturing into the world of authorship has been a fulfilling experience. My writings offer diverse perspectives on life, inviting readers to explore the intricacies of human experience. I Invite fellow writers, readers, and professionals, and welcome your thoughts on this new endeavor. I find solace and inspiration in the world of literature...*

***Instagram**- Oh girl or I call you pearl,*
Beautifully white,
Glowing to sight,
Developed in shell,
But beautiful as hell,
A natural gift of sea,
We are blessed to see,
Shades of golden, black, pink,
Got the eyes, making me sink,
Got an excellent lustre,
Similarly a great gesture,
Not simple but rare,
A thing to preserve and care,
innocence, wisdom, purity,

Some qualities with security,
Simplicity is what you believe,
Beauty is what we receive,
Time and relation making a purl,
Lucky me who got a pearl...

14. Why?- daksh jain

DAKSH JAIN

BIO- As a Computer Science Engineering student, venturing into the world of authorship has been a fulfilling experience. My writings offer diverse perspectives on life, inviting readers to explore the intricacies of human experience. I Invite fellow writers, readers, and professionals, and welcome your thoughts on this new endeavor. I find solace and inspiration in the world of literature...

***Instagram-** @word_by_soul*

WHY to trust ?
when it's not forever,
Easy to burst
And it never recover!
WHY to move ?
When it's not together,
Making a groove
When leaving forever !
WHY to say ?
When it's not heard,
Making you prey
And extracting their word!

WHY this occur ?
When it's not frequent,
Why to bother
When is not meant to be constant.......

15. Passing By- daniel yumkham

Daniel Yumkham

BIO- *Daniel Yumkham, an 18 year old History enthusiast pursuing BA Honours. Despite struggling with stuttering, I've discovered my voice through writing. It's my sanctuary, where words flow freely.*

Instagram- *@daniel_yumkham*

As I pass by the ruined remnants
Of a neighbourhood which had succumbed to war's fury,
Memories of our school van's joyful ride
Through streets now disfigured and barren inside
Linger in my mind.
The lanes where friends once glided like a breeze,
Now stands destroyed, their dreams cast into ether.
Houses that sheltered laughter and dreams,
Now reduced to smoldering embers' gleam.
Their aspirations, burnt with flames,
Leaving only ash and heartfelt pains.
As i search within my heart
On the aftermath of war,
I espy no victory,

But destruction and devastation all around me.
Homes built with love, sweat, and hard-earned money,
All annihilated in an instant;
Centuries-old relationships,
All destroyed in a fleeting moment.
What then, is the benefit of war?
What then, is the benefit of victory?

16. Unrequited Constellations- shaaz

Shaaz

BIO- *: I'm an 18 year old student with a passion for transforming thoughts into poetic masterpieces , I strive to showcase the inherent beauty of words through my work . Crafting verses that captivate and inspire . I aim to share the power and magic of language with the world . Whether exploring themes of love , nature or introspection . I pour my heart and soul into each carefully chosen word , seeking to spark imagination and emotion in all who encounter my creations .*

Instagram- *@inkchanters18*
The Inkenchanter stood beneath the dark night sky
Gazing at the shimmering moon with tears in his eyes
" For when you see the sky , you will think of me" she used to say
But now he knew she would never be his in any way
" You were always too dear for me " he whispered to the stars above
A love unrequited , a soul lost in unending love
" I was always with you , but I couldn't be yours " he sighed
His heart heavy with the weight of unspoken words denied

" I was your tear , your smile and everything you craved
And you were mine , my tear , my smile , everything I've saved "
But was this love only felt by him , a one sided dream?
As he looked upon the sky , his soul torn at the seam
Do you feel what I feel , my dear? " he asked the silent night
A yearning soul searching for a spark of shared light
Everyone fears the pain of unrequited love's sting
But for the Inkenchanter , it was loneliness that clung
To be left unloved , unwanted , by all that he holds dear
A fate too cruel , a heart too shattered to bear
Every word that passed his lips was a quote
A testament to a love lost , a heart's silent note
Inkenchanter , a solitary being lost in his own mind
Longing for a love that seemed impossible to find
As he looked up at the sky with tears in his eyes
He whispered to the stars , " I was always too dear for your skies
"

17. Timeless Love- ahana banerjee

Ahana Banerjee

***BIO**- An ordinary bengali girl weaving her dreams and desires into verses.*

***Instagram**- @ahana_scribbles*

In school, they share their tiffin bites,
Walk to tuition through fading lights.
A glance, a smile—no need for more,
The two tender souls—
For them, this simple love is pure.
The teens—
Their hearts race fast and strong,
Their first kiss felt like a perfect song.
They dream of futures yet untold,
Building their world with love so bold.
As years pass by, love gently grows,
Until in twilight years, their steps are slow.
Though others see them as aged and sheen,
Their wrinkles hide a love that is—
Forever young and green.
Then rain begins, soft as a sigh,

And all the couples gaze at the sky.
They dance as one, in joy's embrace—
Love, Ageless, timeless, fills the space.
Watching them revel in the rain, I hold my beloved's hand,
Pull him close, into the pouring rain,
And join those hearts with a joyful chase.
All smiles, and laughter, and songs, and promises,
This is what love is—
Beyond All Ages.

18. Light green eyes- angel rathi

ANGEL RATHI

BIO- *I write to express myself and my emotions as I think that writting is the best way to express one's feelings and to understand them.*

Instagram- *@angel_rathi*

The light green eyes, the depths behind,
A wall painted by a blend of green-painted lines.
In that gaze, I found something mine,
Something sweet, something kind, so divine.
Those light green eyes looked into mine,
And I knew, in that moment, it was a sign.
The softness in their glow, gentle and bright,
Wrapped around my heart, flooding me with light.
The world paused, and time seemed to unwind,
As the warmth of their presence was all I could find.
In that fleeting moment, where dreams intertwine,
I discovered a love that felt perfectly aligned.
With every glance shared, the magic would grow,
A bond formed in silence, a soft, tender flow.
In the depths of those eyes, I found peace and grace,

A forever etched promise, a sacred embrace.

19. Someone all mine- angel rathi

Angel Rathi

BIO- *I write to express myself and my emotions as I think that writting is the best way to express one's feelings and to understand them.*

Instagram- *@angel_rathi*

Someone all mine,
In a world that feels so wide,
Someone all mine,
In whom I can confide.
Someone all mine,
Through laughter and through tears,
Someone all mine,
To share my hopes and fears.
Someone all mine,
A heart that beats in tune,
Someone all mine,
My sun and my moon.
Someone all mine,
In every whispered word,
Someone all mine,

A bond that's felt, not heard.
Someone all mine,
In moments soft and sweet,
Someone all mine,
My home where two hearts meet.
Someone all mine,
We will grow old with time,
Someone all mine,
We will be together till the end of the line .

20. Forever by your side- angel rathi

Angel Rathi

BIO- *I write to express myself and my emotions as I think that writting is the best way to express one's feelings and to understand them.*

Instagram- *@angel_rathi*

Can't be more grateful ,
Then I am now.
You were born with a light,
Helping me find my way out.
I didn't want to live, but you calm it all down,
Tired of surviving, your smile pulls me back somehow.
Grateful I am for your existence,
I can't deny it, even if I try,
Without you, I would have been gone
Long before my time.
I don't know how, but with you, everything feels right,
It's as if you're my own damn child.
Just remember, you're my hope, my reason to survive—
I was dead before you came to life.

My little sister, I'll always stay by your side,
Protect you until the day I die.
Be someone you'll idolize,
My baby, my little fairy, my reason to live this life.

21. In all i love- angel rathi

Angel Rathi

***BIO**- I write to express myself and my emotions as I think that writting is the best way to express one's feelings and to understand them.*

***Instagram**- @angel_rathi*

I love the sky so vast and blue,
The clouds I love that drift on through.
I love the stars shining so bright,
The moon I love glowing in the night.
I love the rain, its soft embrace,
The books I love that take me to another place.
I love the poems with words so deep,
And the cat I love curled fast asleep.
I love the days with a cheerful hue,
The nights I laugh with my mom, it's true.
I love the music with a comforting tune,
And the work I love that beneath the afternoon .
But more than these, both old and new,
I love you most—yes, I do.
I love this world,

I think it's all beautiful.
In all I love,
I love you.

22. The weight of dying petals- gyayak jain

Gyayak jain

Bio- *Aspiring poet with a fresh, youthful perspective on love andheartbreak. I capture the raw emotions of first love, longing and loss and presents the vulnerability of young hearts navigating relationships by finding solace in words.*
Instagram- *@quotes_by_gyayak & @gyayak_jain_17_12*

In the garden of my soul, where shadows creep,
I tend the roots of sorrow, buried deep.
Each thorny memory, each whispered sigh,
In the stillness of the night, I let them die.
Your bitterness once bloomed, a bitter rose,
Its petals sharp, where once love chose.
But in this quiet haven, I've learned to heal,
With every tear that falls, I slowly feel.
The sun breaks through the clouds of doubt and pain,
As I pull the weeds of anger from the grain.
The fragrance of forgiveness fills the air,
In this sacred space, I find the courage to care.
Though echoes of your laughter haunt the breeze,
I plant new seeds of hope among the trees.

In the garden of my soul, I sow the light,
Letting go of shadows, I embrace the night.
So here I stand, beneath the weeping sky,
With every whispered prayer, I learn to fly.
In the garden of my heart, I bid you farewell,
And nurture blossoms where love can dwell.
Yet still, the weight of petals bruised and torn,
Lingers in the garden where love was born.
The soil remembers every touch, each fall,
But slowly, I rise above it all.
The roots of pain run deep, but I grow tall,
With every passing storm, I feel the call—
To shed the leaves of heartache and regret,
To nurture seeds of love that haven't bloomed yet.
In the quiet moments, when dusk turns gray,
I gather strength to greet another day.
And though your absence still lingers in the air,
My heart finds peace, knowing I can care.

23. Love in the distance- gyayak jain

Gyayak jain

BIO-*Aspiring poet with a fresh, youthful perspective on love and heartbreak. I capture the raw emotions of first love, longing and loss and presents the vulnerability of young hearts navigating relationships*
by finding solace in words.
Instagram- *@quotes_by_gyayak & @gyayak_jain_17_12*

She's the sun, so full of light,
Waking the world with morning's first sight.
But I, the moon, rise when she's gone,
Her day begins just as my night comes on.
She greets the dawn, bright and bold,
While I stay lost in the night's quiet cold.
I wake too late to see her glow,
And by the time she sleeps, I start to show.
She's the warmth that touches the day,
While I bring the stars, and drift far away.
Opposites we are, like fire and ice,
Connected by a distance, but never close twice.
But she's so special, more than she knows,

Without her light, my own never shows.
I reflect her shine, but it's not mine,
Without her warmth, I cease to shine.
For I am the moon, empty and cold,
Without her brightness, I have no hold.
She lights my sky, she makes me whole,
Without her glow, I lose my soul.
Though we're apart, my love won't fade,
Through endless nights, for her, I've prayed.
I orbit her world, bound by a tether,
Hoping one day we'll be closer together.
But deep in my heart, I quietly know,
The sun and the moon can't share the same glow.
Though I'll love her beyond the stars above,
I'm just a shadow in the light of her love.
Eternal, my love, yet lost in her flame,
A distant admirer, without a name.
And so I wait in the silence of night,
Watching her shine from the edge of my sight.
For she'll rise with the dawn, and I'll fade away,
The sky is hers, while I silently stay
Though I love her more than she'll ever see,
We're fated to part, just as we'll always be.

24. Fated to fade- gyayak jain

Gyayak jain

BIO- *Aspiring poet with a fresh, youthful perspective on love and heartbreak. I capture the raw emotions of first love, longing and loss and presents the vulnerability of young hearts navigating relationships*
by finding solace in words.

Instagram- *@quotes_by_gyayak & @gyayak_jain_17_12*

We met in a moment, brief and bright,
Two hearts colliding in borrowed light.
In your smile, I found a place to stay,
But deep down, I knew we'd drift away.
We danced through days that felt like dreams,
But love's not always what it seems.
I loved you then, I love you still,
And even though we part, I always will.
For every touch was like a flame,
Yet time passed on, and we weren't the same.
I reached for you, but you slipped away,
And I'm left with words I'll never say.
The laughter faded, replaced by quiet,

But my heart's a fire you can't deny it.
I love you now, like I loved you then,
Though we're fated to fade again and again.
I watched the distance grow with time,
Each step away, another climb.
But still, I wait with love untold,
For your warmth, in this growing cold.
We whispered dreams, but time moved fast,
Building a future that couldn't last.
I held onto hope as you let go,
Fated to fade, but you'll never know.
You moved on, but I stayed right here,
Carrying your love year after year.
Though the world forgets, I never will,
For I love you now, and I always will.
I see you smile from across the way,
Like nothing between us ever gave way.
But in my chest, the ache remains,
A love that endures, despite the pain.
You'll never know the scars you leave,
The silent nights, the tears I grieve.
But even as we drift apart,
You still hold the keys to my heart.
We were fated to fade, but I won't forget,
The love we shared, the dreams we set.
For though we've gone our separate ways,

OUR OWN WORLD

I'll love you for all my days.
I carry you with me, through time and space,
Your memory etched in every place.
No matter how far you go, I'll stay,
Loving you more with each passing day.
And though you've moved on, as life must do,
In my heart, there's only you.
Fated to fade, but never to end,
I'll love you forever, even as a friend.
So here I stand, alone but true,
With love that never dies for you.
Though time may steal what we once had,
I'll always love you—through the good and the bad.
We were fated to fade, but my love won't cease,
For in you, my heart has found its peace.
Though distance may part us and silence may grow,
My love for you will eternally glow.

25. A Love that never fades- gyayak jain

Gyayak jain

BIO- *Aspiring poet with a fresh, youthful perspective on love and heartbreak. I capture the raw emotions of first love, longing and loss and presents the vulnerability of young hearts navigating relationships*
by finding solace in words.

Instagram- *@quotes_by_gyayak & @gyayak_jain_17_12*

I have loved you, in days long past,
When time moved slowly, and moments would last.
In quiet smiles and secret stares,
In every whispered word we shared.
I loved you in the first hello,
When everything was new, and we didn't yet know
That hearts could beat in perfect tune,
Like summer nights beneath the moon.
I loved you when the world was bright,
When your laughter made the darkness light.
In every touch, in every glance,
In every dream, in every chance.
I have loved you, through storm and sun,

When every battle felt like we had won.
In every hug, in every sigh,
I have loved you, without asking why.
I love you still, in this very day,
Though life has changed and drifted away.
Through all the storms that came our way,
Through silent nights and cloudy days.
I love you now, though time has passed,
Though moments fade, my love will last.
It's in the air, it's in the sound,
In every heartbeat that still pounds.
I love you in the quiet hours,
In whispered hopes and unseen flowers.
Though distance grows and shadows fall,
I love you more through it all.
In every tear that I've held tight,
In every morning, in every night.
I love you now, through loss and gain,
Through every joy, through every pain.
I will always love you, come what may,
Even when time takes you away.
When days grow cold, and stars don't shine,
My love for you will still be mine.
In the years ahead, where paths diverge,
Through every wave, through every surge.
I will love you through the test of time,
Even when we've passed our prime.

When we're but memories in the past,
When all has gone, my love will last.
For love like this doesn't fade away,
It grows stronger with each day.
In every sunset, in every rise,
In the endless depths of the skies.
I'll love you when the world is still,
And even then, I'll love you still.
I have loved you, I love you still,
And I will love you, come what will.
For love like ours transcends all time,
It's forever, an endless rhyme.
In every moment, in every breath,
My love for you will conquer death.
I've loved you then, I love you now,
And I will love you, this is my vow.
No matter where this life will go,
No matter what we'll come to know.
Through every change and every pain,
My love for you will still remain.
So, here I stand, forever true,
For I have loved, and still love you.

26. The dream eve- akshat shevde

AKSHAT SHEVDE

BIO-:- *As a 19-year-old engineering student at VNIT, I weave together the worlds of logic and emotion. My poetry captures the beauty of quiet moments and hidden feelings, a contrast to the structured world of engineering.*

Instagram- *@akshat_versifies*

I sit across from her, trying not to feel,
But her gaze, so soft, makes it hard to conceal.
In the canteen, a look we share,
I tell myself, "Don't you dare."
Her eyes, they speak in a language I fear,
A whisper of love that's all too near.
But I push it away, try to stand tall,
Knowing that to feel is to fall.
Awkward, yet tender, these moments unfold,
As if love's secret story is quietly told.
The rain-soaked streets, a perfect stage,
For a love story that time cannot cage.
Together we walked, side by side,

In the melody of the evening, emotions abide.
Earbuds shared, a song we both adore,
But I know I can't let it become more.
"Tum Se Hi", our voices softly sing,
In that moment, I felt everything.
"Abhi Na Jao," the song softly pleads,
Under the moon, where my heart misleads.
I'm losing the battle, my resolve starts to fade,
For in her presence, my heart has strayed .

27. Jealous- akshat shevde

AKSHAT SHEVDE

BIO-:-*As a 19-year-old engineering student at VNIT, I weave together the worlds of logic and emotion. My poetry captures the beauty of quiet moments and hidden feelings, a contrast to the structured world of engineering.*

Instagram- *@akshat_versifies*

Even the breeze that brushes your hair,
Stirs my jealousy, wishing I were there.
Jealous of the sun that warms your skin,
Yearning to be the glow that draws you in
Jealous of the moon that softly gleams,
Wishing I could be the light in your dreams.
Jealous of the stars that sparkle in view,
Hoping to be the one you wish upon, too.
Jealous of the rain that kisses your skin,
Hoping I could be where you begin.
Jealous of the rain that whispers your name,
I wish I could be the one to feel the same.
Jealous of all that touches you near,
Hoping one day, it will be me you hold dear.

28. The Backup- akshat shevde

AKSHAT SHEVDE

BIO-:-*As a 19-year-old engineering student at VNIT, I weave together the worlds of logic and*
emotion. My poetry captures the beauty of quiet moments and hidden feelings, a contrast to the
structured world of engineering.
Instagram- *@akshat_versifies*

In the gallery of faces, I'm the shadow on the wall,
A silent whisper, waiting for a call.
Not the first note in the melody they sing,
Just the echo, the resonance of everything.
I give them my sun, they offer me shade,
I'm a lighthouse, guiding, but always delayed.
They sail towards harbors, in others they trust,
While I stand firm, watching ships turn to dust.
In their storybook, I'm the forgotten page,
An unread tale, lost to time's cage.
Not the hero they cheer for , but the silent line,
That binds the tale, unseen, yet fine.
They say I'm a part of their cherished plan,

But when choices arise, I'm the last they scan.
For though I'm the thread they often forget,
One day, I'll weave a pattern they'll never regret.
One day, this canvas, painted so plain,
Will be the masterpiece, free from pain

29. Fear of Attachments- Akshat shevde

AKSHAT SHEVDE
BIO- :-*As a 19-year-old engineering student at VNIT, I weave together the worlds of logic and emotion. My poetry captures the beauty of quiet moments and hidden feelings, a contrast to the structured world of engineering.*
Instagram- *@akshat_shevde*

They come like whispers in the night.
Promising warmth , a beacon light .
But I have seen this play, times and again,
When bonds were strong, leaving me in pain.
I've watched them leave, one by one,
Under the same unforgiving sun.
Their words once warm, now cold and dry,
Leaving echoes of goodbye.
Once, a spark broke through the dark,
Made me trust, ignited a spark.
But when I was most exposed,
She vanished, leaving wounds unclosed.

Now, I guard this heart of mine,
Afraid to cross that delicate line.
For each new face, a silent plea—
Please don't be another memory.

30. Love - gargi singh

Gargi Singh

BIO- *My name is gargi singh even though i do use Delaney delers also as my pen name i aspire to be a known poet in the future even though i started to write poems this year only but they have been a place of comfort for me so i look forward to writing more poems in the future.*

Instagram- *@_nightmare_daydream_*

I will love you
I will love you till the end of time
I will love you till the sun stops shining
I will love you till the ocean dries up
I will love you till my death
And even after death my bones decaying
Six feet below ground will have your name
If i become a star i will shine just for you
If i become any celestial being i will be visible just to you
Incase i become a ghost
I will come back to love and haunt you and you only
The day my love dies for you just know my presence is erased
forever from this universe
From your memories......
Even when i say "I hate you"

Just know i am lying
Because i can never hate you with all my heart
For loving you now feels like a hobby
Like a major part of my personality
Even when we are apart and fighting
Know that my heart still loves you
For i will love you till the sun stops shinning
And the ocean dries up.....

31. Mine- gargi singh

Gargi Singh

***BIO-** My name is gargi singh even though i do use Delaney delers also as my pen name i aspire to be a known poet in the future even though i started to write poems this year only but they have been a place of comfort for me so i look forward to writing more poems in the future.*

***Instagram-** @_nightmare_daydream_*

I want to be your only infinity
I want to be your only forever
I want.....NEED to be the only one
You share your heart's desire to
I may sound possessive or toxic.....
But beleive me it is the love i feel for you
That pushes me to feel these emotions too...
Don't talk to anyone else
Don't laugh with anyone else
Don't give your shoulders to rest upon to anyone else
Don't even think about anyone else
If my happiness is a person then
It is you for who else can make me smile
Even when i want to cry so badly
The answer obvious to everyone is you

32. I Give You- gargi singh

Gargi Singh

BIO- *My name is gargi singh even though i do use Delaney delers also as my pen name i aspire to be a known poet in the future even though i started to write poems this year only but they have been a place of comfort for me so i look forward to writing more poems in the future.*

Instagram- *@_nightmare_daydream_*

You are so in demand
That every minute with you in silence seems a waste
And every convo so short that
If i had a hourglass the type
That would let me control how time passes
I would speed up every moment without you
And slow down every moment with you
If i had a frame the type
That would let me decide who is with you
I would put myself and only me with you
for I can't bear the scene of you with someone else
If i had a speaker the type
That would let me decide who you yap to

I would make me the only listener
For i want to be the only one who knows you deep
If i had a camera the type
That would let me decide who sees you
You would be invisible to everyone but me
For i want to be the only one praising your celestial beauty
If I had a cage the type
That would tie you to me that would make you just mine
You would be my prisoner even though i am yours to break and mend
But unfortunately i don't own such things
Neither can i create them
For if i could i would no matter what it took
So i give you these
My trust;break it not for it is of glass
My love; reject it not for then i will be unwilling to keep this emotion anymore
My heart;mend it don't break it for by giving you my heart i also make you my only hope
My tears; don't let them flow for nothing for these will choke me like poison
My happiness;keep it safe for you are the reason

33. "O' Krishna, my lord of this world"- shivang maurya

Shivang maurya

BIO- *I am Shivang Maurya, currently pursuing humanities at the prestigious University of Allahabad, specifically in the Department of European Languages. With a deep passion for languages and literature, I have explored various forms of expression, including romantic, erotic, and ballad poetry, as well as the rich tradition of Hindi ghazals. My love for words has led me to write several books on grammar, aiming to guide and inspire students in mastering language skills.*

As a linguistic guide and literature coach, I find joy in mentoring students, helping them appreciate the beauty of language, and cultivating their abilities to express themselves eloquently. I believe in the transformative power of words and am dedicated to sharing this belief with my students.

I dedicate all my efforts to my beloved parents and my dear students, who continually inspire me to strive for excellence in everything I do.

Instagram- *@skssyntaticseng_01*

O' Lord of this hell,
Made our lives in paradise;
Through your lips on me thy flute,
Needs some breath for my life.
Then press the orifices of my body,
To make the sound like heaven;
Among this noisy world, some melody,
Only I only you in this coffin.
Now, this the darkness turns into light,
Make those clouds from dark to white;
Under the solace of this natural beauty,
Hold my flesh so tight.
O' Lord of this hell,
Made our lives in Paradise.
(Here, 'hell' is referring this material world and Radha is symbolising herself as Lord's servitude, who wants to spend her time with him in the heaven)

34. You're my everything- priyanka pandit

Priyanka Pandit
***BIO**- I just love to write because it'll relax me sometimes and when I cannot express my feelings i just write.*
***Instagram**- @_p.pihu_*

In your words, I find a calm that soothes my restless tide,
Like a lighthouse in the dark, you're my guiding light inside.
Your love is the compass that leads me through the night,
In your embrace, every shadow fades, and everything feels right.

Together we sail, no storm too fierce to face,
In your strength, I find courage, in your heart, a warm embrace.
With you, even the rain becomes a song, so sweet and pure,
In our love, we find a world where every fear has its cure.

Your words are the melody to which my heart will always sway,
In this dance of love, with you, I wish forever to stay.

35. Hey!- mobin

Mobin

BIO- *Hello,I am mobin an free guy who is just trying to figure a way out with the words.I know am not that great of a writer but still, Thanks for taking the time to write my workI am really great full for the opportunity.And ,I haven't figured out my pen name yet so Anyone reading my poem if something comes in your mind make sure to let me know,I would really appreciate. Once again Thanks for this opportunity.*

Instagram- *@mobin1991318114*

It all started with a word
having two letter...
And,after that the day
The life became, So much better
Its hard to explain ...
The way brain has more complaints
But the heart wins every time
Because....
for now you are just mine!!

36. Flames that Flickers- R. subash sai sudhan

***

R. Subash sai sudhan
BIO- *An 18 year old, studies at SA college of science & arts, who started writing to express his love to his muse.*
Instagram- *@sudhan_unscripted & @sr7_online*

Echoes of memories, your name remains
A bittersweet reminder of love's fleeting flames
Distance and time took their toll
Leaving shadows, where love once made me whole
I'll hold on to the love we shared
A flame that flickers, though you're no longer there

37. Promise made- R. subash sai sudhan

R. Subash sai sudhan
BIO- An 18 year old, studies at SA college of science & arts, who started writing to express his love to his muse.
Instagram- @sudhan_unscripted & @sr7_online

Met by accident, chose to be together
Differences arose, yet promised forever
An unbreakable bond, forged by love and affection
Yet some toxic person disturbed it like an infection
A promise made, to safeguard the heart
One will step back, to play a brand new part
Love's bond remains, though physically apart
Forever entwined, in heart

38. Forever yours, Never mine- sanvi jaiswal

SANVI JAISWAL

BIO-*"Sanvi, a 15-year-old wordsmith in progress, weaves emotions into verse. A poet and seeker of truth, I share my story from heart to page. I invite you, dear readers, to join this little poet's journey."*

***Instagram-** @alfaaz.ankahe_se*
She loves him,
knowing he'll never be her's to hold,
A heart that beats for him alone
Though he'll never love her the same,
Her heart remains, forever in flames
She knows he'll never hold her tight,
Yet, her heart beats for him day & night
Longing to be close to his side,
To feel his warmth his gentle pride
But alas, fate has other plans
leaving her with empty hands
Still she holds on to the thought,
of what could've been, what's been brought

A love so strong, yet impossible to claim,
A heart that loves, despite the pain

39. Love is not a game- joy pannu

Joy Pannu

BIO- *A 13 year old, who just loves to write poems.*
Instagram- *@joy_poems.13*

" 'LOVE' is not a Game
it's a connection of Brain
Sometimes it's like.....
Anxiety, Depression and Pain
No one can get love !!
through Force and Fame
love displays pictures of Life
with the Beauty of in a Light
without love life is Worse !
if you still think love is a game
then you must think again...... "

40. I hate roses- Chrysolyte

CHRYSOLYTE
Instagram- *@_scribblemymess_*

I hate roses, they mock what I feel,
Blood-red lies, pretending they heal.
They told me it was love, but what's the deal?
Every petal just hid a wound that wouldn't seal.
People said roses were perfect, pure bliss,
But no one warned me about the thorns I'd miss.
How they cut me deep when I leaned in to kiss,
Leaving scars that still scream, "Remember this."
They gave them at wedding, like love was the prize,
But roses rot fast, just like the lies.
I heard "forever", then watched as it died,
And I was left wondering why everyone cries.
I hate roses, they withered in days,
Just like the promises thrown in my face.
They were beautiful, sure, but beauty decays,
And all I'm left with is the pain that stays.
So, tell me – what's more cruel, the bloom or the fade?
Is it the petals I cherished, or the wounds they made?

Maybe I chased the hurt that was never explained...
But if you know this isn't about roses,
Then, why am I still the one bleeding from the blade

41. The one that got away- suhana saha

Suhana Saha

BIO- *I'm Suhana Saha, a 21-year-old law student from Kurseong, West Bengal. I've discovered a passion for writing poetry, which helps me express my feelings and connect with others. With two published poems, I'm excited to continue writing from the heart, sharing my thoughts and experiences freely.*

Instagram- *@suhana_.2003*

I fell for him before we met,
A love I'll never fully forget.
They call me foolish; how could it be,
To love someone I would never see?
But they don't know the way he smiled,
His pretty eyes, the way he is shy.
He teased me gently, made me smile,
As if the miles didn't matter a while.
He listened when I needed him,
Gossiped, laughed, made me feel like a dream.
We didn't need to meet face to face,
He made me feel happy and safe.

It hurts that we're not meant to stay,
That life has pulled us separate ways.
Though we weren't meant to find a way,
But still, he means the world to me.
I may not move on, and that's okay,
He deserves joy in every way.
I'll never hate him, never forget,
He is a part of me, no regret.
Maybe in another world, we'd choose
Each other, without the fear to lose.
But in this life, I'll just be glad,
For the love we had, for the memories we have.

42. One heart, One soul- lovejeet sharma

Lovejeet sharma

BIO- *My pen name is Shayar a young college student who has god gifted ability to write verses about love,god, loyalty...etc once I get any respected job I will learn professional writting skills and bang whole industry.*

Instagram- *@love_jeet78603*

This is the story of our every night
We two are the same part of the night
Like the moon, stars, wind and silence
Oh! Dear There is just only a love of souls
We don't know what prostitution is
Only a trickster lover know this
Oh dear let them joy their fake love
We both are not that kind of lover
Oh dear our love isn't Gen z kinda love
Our love is of one heart and one soul
Our love is of one heart and one soul